CW00430412

A DISH FOR A WISH
35 CHEFS & CELEBRITIES
35 FABULOUS RECIPES

BROUGHT TO YOU BY
RAYS OF SUNSHINE
CHILDREN'S CHARITY

First published 2012 in Great Britain
by Rays of Sunshine Children's Charity
Registered Charity No. 1102529

Rays of Sunshine Children's Charity
No. 1 Olympic Way
Wembley
Middlesex HA9 0NP
Telephone 020 8782 1171
Fax 020 8782 1173
raysofsunshine.org.uk
info@raysofsunshine.org.uk

A CIP record of this book is available at the British Library

ISBN 978-0-9572474-0-6

Project concept by Laura Barnett
Edited by Laura Barnett,
Rays of Sunshine Children's Charity

Designed by Em-Project Limited
Telephone 01892 614 346
mike@em-project.com
em-project.com

Printed by Butler Tanner and Dennis

Rays of Sunshine would like to thank:
Laura Barnett for her passion in turning this cook book into a tasty reality; our celebrity supporters who have contributed to this book; Mike Turner for helping to make this book possible.

Thanks to Cory Bros for their generous sponsorship of this book.

Rays of Sunshine Children's Charity grants wishes for seriously ill children in the UK aged 3-18.

Every day of the year the charity gives brave and deserving young people the chance to put their illness on hold and enjoy a magical moment.

Welcome to Rays of Sunshine's first cookbook. All the profits from A Dish for a Wish will help our charity to continue granting magical wishes every day for seriously ill children.

There are 20,000 children in the UK living with a serious or life limiting illness. Our mission is to bring a ray of sunshine into as many of these young lives as we can. We create individual wishes, hospital play days and hospital ward wishes. We try to replace fear and sadness with excitement and joy.

Whether granting individual wishes, entertaining children in hospitals or hosting large scale events, our charity touches the lives of thousands of children each year.

Celebrity wishes are obviously a big part of our work and we are so grateful to all our famous supporters who have contributed the delicious recipes that fill this book. You've some scrumptious treats in store.

A Dish for a Wish is dedicated to the courageous children and their families who we are privileged to share poignant moments with every day.

Thank you for buying this book. With the help of supporters like you, Rays of Sunshine can continue to grant magical wishes every day of the year.

If you'd like to buy further copies for friends or take part in one of our many fundraising opportunities, please visit the Rays of Sunshine website www.raysofsunshine.org.uk

Jane Sharpe
Chief Executive
Rays of Sunshine Children's Charity

Leading patisserie chef Lorraine Pascale owns her own successful Covent Garden bakery, Ella's Bakehouse. She also writes for prominent food publications. Her two primetime cookery series on BBC2 attracted millions of viewers and her two cookery books were both bestsellers.

I am proud to be an ambassador for Rays of Sunshine. Being involved has given me firsthand experience of the wonderful work the charity does every day. Whether a child wants to go on a family holiday, visit Disneyworld, own an iPad, be a car park attendant or meet a favourite celebrity, Rays of Sunshine works hard to make that wish come true. Every recipe in A Dish for a Wish has been donated with love by some of the UK's best loved celebrities and chefs. I hope the book will brighten up your kitchen, as every copy sold will help to brighten up the life of a seriously ill child in the UK.

Lorraine Pascale
Ambassador

pp12

pp16

pp18

pp20

pp24

pp28

pp32

pp34

pp36

pp38

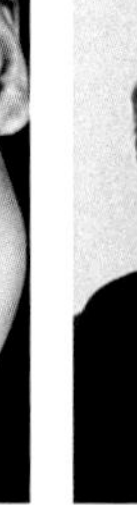
pp40

pp44

pp48

pp50

pp54

pp56

pp60

pp62

pp64

pp66

pp78

pp90

pp102

pp70

pp80

pp94

pp104

pp72

pp82

pp96

pp108

pp76

pp86

pp98

pp110

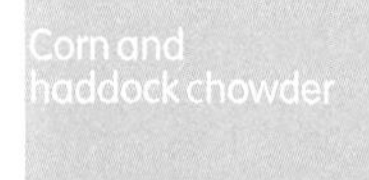

Jollof rice with chicken
Smartie cookies
pp66
pp78
pp90
pp102
Chestnut and vegetable burgers
Custard tart
Mixed fruit pavlova
pp70
pp80
pp94
pp104
Delia's banana and walnut loaf
Apple crumble
pp72
pp82
pp96
pp108
Apple and cinnamon muffins
Lemon posset
pp76
pp86
pp98
pp110

—SMOKED HADDOCK OMELETTE

from Tom Kerridge
Serves 6

—SMOKED HADDOCK OMELETTE

from Tom Kerridge, The Hand & Flowers
Serves 6

—Ingredients

—500g smoked haddock
—570ml milk
—2 cloves
—2 bay leaves
—parsley stalks
—1 onion, chopped
—300g butter
—30g flour
—salt and pepper
—6 egg yolks
—3 shallots, chopped
—4 cloves black pepper
—tarragon stalks
—200ml white wine vinegar
—100ml white wine
—10 eggs
—200g grated parmesan

—Method

—In a pan bring the milk, cloves, bay leaves, parsley stalks and onion up to the boil.
—Remove from the heat and leave to infuse.
—Reduce down the white wine, white wine vinegar, black pepper and tarragon stalks to a glaze and leave to cool.
—Bring the milk back up to simmer and place the smoked haddock in. Take the pan off the heat and allow the fish to gently cook and cool down.
—Blend 10 eggs and pass through a chinoise.
—Take the haddock out of the milk and flake the fish.
—Pass the milk mix into a saucepan and heat. In a separate pan melt 30g of butter then add the flour and cook the roux out.
—Slowly add the milk mix, whisking the whole time.
—When made and cooked out remove from heat.
—Make a hollandaise sauce with the shallot reduction, 2 egg yolks and 250g of melted butter. In blinis pans cook the blended egg mix until just soft.
—Then add the flaked haddock, sprinkle with the grated parmesan.
—Mix together 1 tbsp of béchamel with 1 tbsp of hollandaise and one egg yolk per person.
—Spoon this mix on top of the haddock and glaze under the grill.
—Serve in the blinis pans.

—**CHILLI CON CARNE**
from Rochelle Wiseman
Serves 4

—**Ingredients**
—1 tbsp oil
—1 large onion
—1 red pepper
—2 garlic cloves, peeled
—1 tsp hot chilli powder (or 1 tbsp mild)
—1 tsp paprika
—1 tsp ground cumin
—500g lean minced beef
—1 beef stock cube
—400g can chopped tomatoes
—½ tsp dried marjoram
—1 tsp sugar
—2 tbsp tomato purée
—410g can red kidney beans
—200g long grain rice
—Soured cream to serve

—**Method**
—Chop the onion into small dice, about 5mm square. De-seed and chop the red pepper. Finely chop the garlic cloves.
—Put a large pan on the hob over a medium heat. Add the oil and leave for 1-2 minutes until hot. Add the onions and cook for about 5 minutes, stirring fairly frequently, until the onions are soft, squidgy and slightly translucent. Tip in the garlic, red pepper, chilli powder, paprika and ground cumin. Give it a good stir, then leave to cook for another 5 minutes, stirring occasionally.
—Turn the heat up a bit, add the meat to the pan and break it up with your spoon or spatula. The mix should sizzle a bit when you add the mince. Keep stirring and prodding for at least 5 minutes until all the meat is in uniform lumps and there are no more pink bits. Make sure you keep the heat hot enough for the meat to fry and become brown, rather than just stew.
—Crumble the beef stock cube into 300ml hot water. Pour this into the pan with the mince mixture. Add the chopped tomatoes. Tip in the dried marjoram and sugar. Add a good shake of salt and pepper. Squirt in about 2 tbsp tomato purée and stir the sauce well.
—Bring the whole thing to the boil, give it a good stir and put a lid on the pan. Turn down the heat until it is gently bubbling and leave for 20 minutes. You should check the pan occasionally to give the chilli a stir and make sure the sauce isn't drying out or catching on the bottom. If it is, add a couple of tablespoons of water and make sure that the heat is low enough. After simmering gently, the saucy mince mixture should look thick, moist and juicy.
—Bring on the beans. Drain and rinse the kidney beans in a sieve and stir them into the chilli pot. Bring to the boil again, and gently bubble without the lid for another 10 minutes, adding a little more water if it looks too dry. Season to taste. It will probably take a lot more seasoning than you think. Now replace the lid, turn off the heat and leave your chilli to stand for 10 minutes before serving. Leaving your chilli to stand is really important as it allows the flavours to mingle.
—Serve with soured cream and plain boiled long grain rice.

—CORN AND HADDOCK CHOWDER
from Gregg Wallace
Serves 4

"Not for the faint hearted this one, a chowder is the daddy of soups. I always make loads of this. A big bowl left in my fridge diminishes over a day or two. This is comfort eating. Forget popcorn, this is the perfect accompaniment to a good film."

—Ingredients
—2 sweet corn cobs
—2 potatoes
—2 tbsp olive oil
—25g butter
—1 onion, finely chopped
—1 stalk celery, finely chopped
—300ml fish stock
—100ml white wine
—300g undyed haddock, skinned and cut into 2.5cm chunks
—100ml double cream
—black pepper
—1 bunch parsley, chopped

—Method
—Hold the cobs upright and slice off the yellow kernels.
—Quarter the potatoes and slice each quarter into five. Keep the slices in cold water.
—Heat the oil and butter in a large heavy bottomed pan over a low heat. Add the onion and celery and cook, lid on, for 5 minutes.
—Add the corn kernels and potatoes and cook, lid on, for 10 minutes, stirring occasionally. Don't break up the potatoes.
—Pour in the fish stock and wine, put the lid on, turn up the heat and bring to the boil. Reduce the heat and simmer for five minutes.
—Add the fish, bring to the boil, then simmer, lid on, for 3 minutes, until the fish is cooked. Remove from the heat.
—Stir in the cream and tons of black pepper.
—Serve in bowls and sprinkle with chopped parsley.

—BEEF WELLINGTON
from Gordon Ramsay
Serves 4

—BEEF WELLINGTON

from Gordon Ramsay
Serves 4

—Ingredients

- —400g flat cap mushrooms, roughly chopped
- —sea salt and freshly ground black pepper
- —1-2 tbsp olive oil
- —750g piece prime beef fillet
- —1-2 tbsp English mustard
- —6-8 slices Parma ham
- —500g ready-made puff pastry
- —flour to dust
- —2 egg yolks, beaten

From **Ramsay's Best Menus**
By Gordon Ramsay
Quadrille, £20

—Method

—Pulse the mushrooms in a food processor with some seasoning to a rough paste. Scrape the paste into a pan and cook over a high heat for 8-10 minutes, tossing frequently, to cook out the moisture from the mushrooms. Spread out on a plate to cool.

—Heat a frying pan and add the olive oil. Season the beef and sear in a hot pan for 30 seconds only on each side – just enough to colour it. Remove the beef from the pan and leave to cool, then brush all over with the mustard.

—Lay a sheet of cling film on a work surface and arrange the Parma ham slices on it, in slightly overlapping rows. With a palette knife, spread the mushroom paste over the ham, then place the seared beef fillet in the middle. Keeping hold of the cling film from the edge, neatly roll the Parma ham and mushrooms around the beef to form a tight barrel shape. Twist the ends of the cling film to secure. Chill for 15-20 minutes to allow the beef to set and keep its shape.

—Roll out the puff pastry on a lightly floured surface to a large rectangle, the thickness of a £1 coin. Remove the cling film from the beef, then lay it in the centre of the pastry. Brush the surrounding pastry with egg yolk. Fold the ends over, then wrap the pastry around the beef, cutting off any excess. Turn over, so the seam is underneath, and place on a baking sheet

—Brush the pastry all over with the beaten egg and chill for about 15 minutes to let the pastry rest. Heat the oven to 200°C.

—Lightly score the pastry at 1cm intervals and glaze again with egg. Bake for 20 minutes, then lower the oven setting to 180°C and cook for another 15 minutes. Allow to rest for 10-15 minutes before slicing and serving. The beef should still be pink in the centre when you serve it.

—SESAME TOFU WITH STIR FRIED VEGETABLES

from Leona Lewis
Serves 2-4

—Ingredients

—400g firm tofu
—60ml soy sauce
—1 tbsp dark sesame oil
—1 tbsp rice vinegar
—2 tsp sugar
—2 tsp sesame seeds
—1 x 2.5cm piece fresh ginger
—2 spring onions
—1 clove garlic
—230g snow peas
—3 tbsp vegetable oil
—2 tbsp water
—100-200g white or brown rice, for serving

—Method

—Drain the tofu and cut into 2.5cm cubes. Whisk soy sauce, sesame oil, vinegar and sugar in a glass pie plate or baking dish. Add tofu, turn the coat, and set aside for 30 minutes.

—Meanwhile, toast the sesame seeds in a small dry skillet over medium heat, stirring and tossing, until fragrant and a shade or two darker, about 4 minutes. Pour into a bowl to cool.

—Peel and grate the ginger. Trim and chop the spring onions, keeping the white and green parts separate. Smash, peel and finely chop the garlic. Pull off the stems and any tough strings from the snow peas, if necessary.

—When you're ready to cook the tofu, reserve 1 tbsp of the marinade in a small bowl and drain off the rest. Pat the tofu dry with paper towels.

—Heat 2 tbsp oil in a large nonstick skillet or wok over medium-high to high heat. Working in batches if necessary, fry the tofu in the skillet, turning occasionally, until golden, about 7 minutes. Transfer the tofu with a slotted spoon or spatula; toss with the sesame seeds. Set aside.

—Add the remaining oil to the skillet. Stir-fry the ginger, garlic and spring onion whites until fragrant, about 30 seconds. Add the snow peas and water and stir-fry until the snow peas are bright green and lightly glazed, about 2 minutes.

—Return the fried tofu and spring onion to the pan, pour in reserved marinade, and stir gently to combine. Cook until the snow peas are crisp-tender, about 2 minutes more.

—Serve with rice.

"THE CHARITY HAS A VERY SPECIAL PLACE IN MY HEART AND I AM PRIVILEGED TO BE AN AMBASSADOR. SO MANY CHILDREN IN THE UK ARE BATTLING A SERIOUS ILLNESS AND IT'S SO IMPORTANT TO BE ABLE TO ADD A TOUCH OF SPARKLE INTO THEIR LIVES."

eona Lewis

—FRESH PASTA SERVED WITH CHICKEN AND DOLCELATTE SAUCE

from Gino D'Acampo

Serves 4

—FRESH PASTA SERVED WITH CHICKEN AND DOLCELATTE SAUCE

from Gino D'Acampo
Serves 4

—Ingredients

—400g fresh fettuccine or tagliatelle
—350g chicken breast, boneless and skinless, cut into thin strips
—200g dolcelatte cheese, cut into chunks
—50ml dry white wine
—150ml double cream
—3 tbsp chopped chives
—2 tbsp olive oil
—salt and pepper to taste

—Method

—Heat the oil in a medium size saucepan over a medium heat and fry the chicken for 6 minutes until golden all over, stirring occasionally with a wooden spoon.
—Add in the dolcelatte, lower the heat and cook for 2 minutes stirring until melted.
—Pour in the cream and wine and continue to cook for a further minute stirring continuously.
—Mix in the chives and season with salt and plenty of black pepper. Remove from the heat and set aside.
—Meanwhile, cook the pasta in a large saucepan of salted boiling water until al dente.
—Once the pasta is cooked, drain and tip back into the same pan where you cooked it.
—Pour in the creamy chicken sauce and stir everything together, away from the heat, for 30 seconds allowing the sauce to coat the pasta beautifully.
—Serve immediately.

From **Gino's Pasta**
By Gino D'Acampo
Kyle Cathie, £16.99
Photograph by Kate Whitaker

—CHICKEN CHOW MEIN

by Jameela Jamil
Serves 2

—Ingredients

—400g chicken
—tamari sauce
—garlic
—olive oil
—2 red onions
—300g asparagus
—300g broccoli
—cashew nuts
—vermicelli rice noodles

—Method

—Stir fry cashews, onions and garlic for a minute in olive oil, then add chicken. Once it starts to brown on the outside, add the veg.
—Once cooked, add rice noodles and tamari sauce. Stir for a few minutes until crispy and cooked to taste.
—Short, sweet and even better cold the next day for your packed lunch!

—FISH PIE
from Claudia Winkleman
Serves 4

—Ingredients
—1kg firm white fish (filleted weight)
—a little butter for the dish
—500ml milk
—a bay leaf
—6 black peppercorns
—a little nutmeg
—75g butter
—40g flour
—1 small bunch dill, chopped
—5 stalks bushy parsley
—2 medium leeks

For the potato topping
—5 large potatoes, peeled and diced
—28g butter
—50ml milk

—Method
—Boil the potatoes until soft and mash with the milk and butter. Add salt and pepper.
—Check the fish for any stray bones Lightly butter a baking dish or shallow pan, place the fish in it, and pour over the milk, topping up with a little water to just cover the fish. Add the bay leaf, peppercorns and a very fine grating of nutmeg. Place over a moderate heat, turning it down just before the milk boils. Leave to simmer gently for 5-10 minutes, until the fish is opaque and tender.
—Turn off the heat, remove the fish and strain the liquor to remove the bay leaf. Remove the skin from the fish and discard. Break the fish into large pieces and roughly chop the dill.
—Melt 40g of butter in a saucepan, add the flour and cook till pale biscuit-coloured, stirring almost constantly. Pour in the strained cooking liquid from the fish (adding more, if necessary, to make 500ml), stirring over a moderate heat till smooth. Cook over a low heat for 10 minutes, then fold in the fish. Season with salt, pepper, dill and parsley.
—While the sauce is cooking, slice the leeks thinly, give them a thorough rinse, then let them cook with 35g butter in a deep pan, covered with a lid, until they are soft. It is important that they don't colour, so I often put a round of greaseproof paper on top of the leeks and cover with a lid, which will encourage them to steam.
—Gently fold the cooked leeks into the fish sauce, then transfer to an ovenproof dish.
—Set the oven at 180°C.
—Bake for 40 minutes in the preheated oven until crisp and golden, and the filling is bubbling.

—NACHOS GRANDE

from One Direction
Serves 4

—Ingredients

—450g ground beef
—1 medium onion, chopped
—1 chopped green pepper
—240ml water
—seasoning: salt, pepper, Tabasco, Worcestershire sauce, chilli powder
—225g tortilla chips
—225g grated cheddar cheese
—1 green jalapeno pepper

—Method

—Preheat oven to 190°C. Cook the ground beef, onion and pepper in a large frying pan on medium heat for 5 minutes or until cooked through, stirring frequently. Drain if needed, then add seasoning. Simmer for 5 minutes, stirring occasionally.
—Arrange tortilla chips in a single layer on two lightly greased foil-lined shallow baking pans, overlapping chips if needed to cover the bottom completely. Top each pan of chips with half each of the meat mixture and the cheese.
—Bake for 5 minutes or until the cheese is melted.
—Serve immediately.

—BEEF AND GUINNESS STEW

from Christine Bleakley
Serves 6

"This warming stew is delicious served with mashed potatoes."

—Ingredients

—1kg beef stewing steak
—3 tbsp vegetable oil
—2 tbsp plain flour
—salt and freshly ground black pepper to taste
—1 pinch cayenne pepper
—2 large onions, chopped
—1 clove garlic, crushed
—2 tbsp tomato puree
—375ml Guinness
—3 carrots, chopped
—1 sprig fresh thyme
—1 tbsp chopped fresh parsley to garnish

—Method

—Toss the beef with 1 tbsp of vegetable oil. In a separate bowl, stir together the flour, salt, pepper and cayenne pepper. Dredge the beef in this to coat.

—Heat the remaining oil in a deep frying pan or casserole over medium-high heat. Add the beef and brown on all sides. Add the onions and garlic. Stir the tomato puree into a small amount of water to dilute; pour into the pan and stir to blend. Reduce the heat to medium, cover and cook for 5 minutes.

—Pour one third of the stout into the pan, and as it begins to boil, scrape any bits of food from the bottom of the pan with a wooden spoon. This adds a lot of flavour to the stock. Pour in the rest of the stout and add the carrots and thyme. Cover, reduce heat to low and simmer for 2 to 3 hours, stirring occasionally. Taste and adjust seasoning before serving. Garnish with chopped parsley.

Recipe by **want2hike**

—INSALATA DI BACCALA (SALT COD SALAD)

from Antonio Carlucccio
Serves 6-7

—INSALATA DI BACCALA (SALT COD SALAD)

from Antonio Carluccio
Serves 6-7

—Ingredients

—50g baccala (salt cod)
—2 garlic cloves, crushed
—100g black olives, pitted
—2 tbsp coarsely chopped flat leaf parsley
—6 tbsp olive oil
—juice of 1½ lemons
—freshly ground black pepper

—Method

—Cut the fish into chunks, then soak in cold water for 48 hours, changing the water occasionally. (This soaking is best done skin-side up, as it enables the salt to fall to the bottom of the container.)
—After soaking the fish, drain it and put it in a pan. Cover with fresh cold water, bring to the boil and cook until soft and flaky, about 20 minutes. Drain, and leave to cool.
—Using your fingers, remove all the skin and bones from the salt cod pieces, and reduce the flesh to flakes. Put the fish flakes in a bowl together with the garlic, olives, parsley, olive oil and lemon juice and season with plenty of black pepper. Mix well and serve either on its own or with some good bread.

From **Two Greedy Italians**
By Antonio Carluccio
and Gennaro Contaldo
Quadrille, £20
Photography by Chris Terry

—CRUNCHY CHICKEN BREASTS WITH A PERI PERI, GARLIC AND LEMON ZEST CRUST

from JLS

Serves 4

PUMA

"WE LOVE SUPPORTING RAYS OF SUNSHINE AND HAVE MET HUNDREDS OF INCREDIBLE YOUNG PEOPLE. EVERY ONE OF THESE CHILDREN HAS INSPIRED US WITH THEIR BRAVERY AND COURAGE."

JLS

—CRUNCHY CHICKEN BREASTS WITH A PERI PERI, GARLIC AND LEMON ZEST CRUST

from JLS
Serves 4

—Ingredients

—4 skinless chicken breasts, flattened
—250g Panko breadcrumbs
—zest and juice of 2 lemons
—40g butter
—1 tbsp flat leaf parsley
—salt and freshly ground black pepper to taste
—3 tbsp cake flour
—3 tbsp peri peri sauce
—2 eggs

Peri peri sauce

—10-12 birdseye chillies, chopped finely (medium size, medium heat)
—1 pinch salt
—juice of ½ lemon
—100ml olive oil
—2 tbsp garlic powder (not crushed garlic as the mixture will be too runny)

—Method

—Preheat oven to 180°C.
—Mix all peri peri ingredients together for peri peri sauce.
—Sprinkle the flour onto a plate.
—Beat eggs and peri peri sauce together with lemon zest, parsley and a pinch of salt and pepper.
—Dip each chicken breast into the flour until both sides are completely coated then dip into the egg mixture until covered.
—Dip into the Panko breadcrumbs, making sure the breasts are completely coated.
—Place chicken on a baking tray and bake in the oven for 15-20 minutes.
—Leave breasts whole or slice in strips and drizzle with lemon juice.

—SWEET POTATO SHEPHERD'S PIE

from Daisy Lowe
Serves 4

—Ingredients

—700g ground beef
—1 onion, chopped
—6 mushrooms
—2 carrots, diced
—700g-1kg potatoes
—120g butter
—1 tsp Worcestershire sauce
—1 tin tomatoes
—few drops of Tabasco
—salt, pepper, other seasonings of choice

—Method

—Peel and quarter potatoes, boil in salted water until tender (about 20 minutes).
—While the potatoes are cooking, melt 60g butter in a large frying pan.
—Sauté onions in butter until tender over medium heat for 10 minutes. If you are adding vegetables, add them according to cooking time. Put the carrots in with the onions. Add mushrooms when the meat has initially cooked.
—Add ground beef and sauté until no longer pink. Add mushrooms, seasoning and the tin of tomatoes. Cook uncovered over low heat for 10 minutes,
—Mash potatoes in a bowl with the remainder of the butter. Season to taste.
—Place beef and onions in a baking dish. Distribute mashed potatoes on top. Rough up with a fork so that there are peaks that will brown nicely. You can use the fork to make some designs in the potatoes as well.
—Cook in 170°C oven until bubbling and brown (about 30 minutes). Grill for last few minutes if necessary to brown.

Photography by Niclas Heikkinen
for Indie Magazine

—7 HOUR SLOW ROAST SHOULDER OF LAMB WITH ONIONS, THYME AND BALSAMIC VINEGAR

from Tom Aikens

—7 HOUR SLOW ROAST SHOULDER OF LAMB WITH ONIONS, THYME AND BALSAMIC VINEGAR

from Tom Aikens
Serves 6

—Ingredients

The lamb

- —2.5kg shoulder of lamb
- —1 small bunch thyme, washed
- —8 medium onions, peeled
- —2 bulbs garlic, peeled
- —350ml balsamic vinegar
- —2g sea salt
- —150ml olive oil

The mashed potato

- —2 litres water
- —20g salt
- —350g butter
- —400ml warmed milk
- —1kg potatoes, peeled
- —12 turns of milled black pepper

—Method

—Depending on when you are going to be eating this dish – either lunch or dinner – put it into the oven a meal before. So for lunch, put it into the oven at 8am, and for the evening put it in at around 2pm. It will take between 6-7 hours to cook, but it is one of those dishes that do not need any attention at all.

—Before you cook the lamb, leave it out of the fridge for a good hour or two so the meat is at room temperature. Rub on a little olive oil and season with salt and pepper. Place a little olive oil into the bottom of the pan with the onions, then lay the lamb on top. Put it into the oven at 180°C for 15-20 minutes until the lamb and onions have coloured.

—Remove the pot from the oven, then add about 8 sprigs of thyme along with the garlic, turn the oven down to 100-110°C and cook this for 5 hours with a lid on.

—Remove the garlic and onions from the pan and place onto a tray, add the balsamic vinegar and remove the lid and continue to cook for a further 1-1½ hours, basting the shoulder in the vinegar every 20 minutes. Remove the pan from the oven and place onto a low heat to reduce any excess liquid that is in the pan and baste the lamb in this whilst it is reducing. Add the onions and garlic back to the pan for 10 minutes to reheat and serve with the mashed potato.

—Cut the potato into 5cm pieces and rinse in cold water, place into a pan with the water and 16g of salt, place onto the heat and bring to a slow simmer. Simmer for 25-35 minutes till they are just tender, tip the potatoes into a colander to drain well. Place the potatoes into a moulis, adding the butter, or mash with a potato masher, adding the butter. Place back into the pan, adding the remaining salt, milled pepper and warm milk.

t at all.
Harr
Ho

—JOHNNY'S SPICY MEATBALLS

from Johnny Vaughan
Serves 6

—Ingredients

Meatballs

- —400g ground beef
- —150g ground pork
- —1 small onion, finely chopped, or a couple of shallots
- —50g breadcrumbs
- —coriander, finely chopped (about an egg cup full)
- —1 tbsp Worcestershire sauce
- —a little flour

Tomato sauce

- —olive oil
- —1 clove garlic, crushed
- —1 onion, finely chopped
- —tomato puree
- —1 large tin chopped tomatoes
- —4 Sicilian plum tomatoes
- —cheap chianti
- —white sugar
- —coriander, finely chopped for garnish
- —spaghetti to serve

—Method

- —Combine all of the meatball ingredients, shape into small balls and roll in flour.
- —Fry off meatballs until brown in a little oil and set aside.
- —Put olive oil into pan and add the onion and garlic until softened.
- —Add tomato puree, both lots of tomatoes, chianti and a little white sugar and simmer for 15 minutes.
- —Add the meatballs back into the pan and continue to simmer for another 15 minutes.
- —Serve with spaghetti and sprinkled with coriander.

—TURKEY CHILLI
from Lisa Snowdon
Serves 6

"Turkey chilli is yummy, quick and fun to make. Add grated cheese, chopped avocado, sour cream and tortilla chips at the end, all over rice or on a jacket spud."

—Ingredients
—1½ tsp olive oil
—450g ground turkey
—1 onion, chopped
—500ml water
—1 tin crushed tomatoes
—1 tin kidney beans, drained, rinsed and mashed
—1 tbsp garlic, minced
—2 tbsp chilli powder
—½ tsp paprika
—½ tsp dried oregano
—½ tsp ground cayenne pepper
—½ tsp ground cumin
—½ tsp salt
—½ tsp ground black pepper

—Method
—Heat the oil in a large pot over medium heat. Place the turkey in the pot and cook until evenly brown. Stir in the onion and cook until tender.
—Pour the water into the pot. Mix in the tomatoes, kidney beans and garlic. Season with the chilli powder, paprika, oregano, cayenne pepper, cumin, salt and pepper.
—Bring to a boil.
—Reduce heat to low, cover and simmer for 30 minutes.

"RAYS OF SUNSHINE IS AN INSPIRATIONAL CHARITY WHICH BRIGHTENS UP THE LIVES OF SERIOUSLY ILL CHILDREN IN THE UK BY GRANTING WISHES. IT HAS BEEN MY PRIVILEGE TO MEET SOME INCREDIBLE YOUNG PEOPLE THROUGH THE CHARITY."

Lisa Snowdon

—CHICKEN MILANESE WITH TOPPINGS

from Gwyneth Paltrow
Serves 4

—Ingredients

—4 boneless, skinless chicken breasts
—250ml milk
—500ml plain breadcrumbs
—salt & pepper to taste
—60ml extra virgin olive oil

Slow-roasted cherry tomatoes and arugula topping

—16-20 cherry tomatoes
—2 tbsp extra virgin olive oil
—kosher salt to taste
—500ml arugula
—1 tbsp balsamic vinegar

Tomato and avocado salad topping

—1 avocado, diced
—8 cherry tomatoes, quartered
—3 spring onions, chopped
—1 tbsp coriander, chopped
—1 tbsp extra virgin olive oil
—juice of 1 lime

—Method

—Place the chicken breasts between two pieces of wax paper, and pound until very thin. Place the milk in a shallow dish, and the breadcrumbs, salt and pepper in another shallow dish. Dip each piece of chicken in the milk, then dredge in the breadcrumbs. Shake off any excess. Heat the olive oil in a large non-stick skillet. Cook two breasts at a time, about 4 minutes on the first side, 2-3 minutes after flipping. Wipe the skillet and repeat for the other two breasts.

Slow-roasted cherry tomatoes and arugula topping

—Preheat the oven to 200°C. Toss the cherry tomatoes with 1 tbsp of olive oil and the salt to taste. Place in a baking dish. Roast for 45 minutes, stirring occasionally – the skins should be blistered and split. Toss the arugula with 1 tbsp of olive oil, the balsamic vinegar and a pinch of salt. Add the tomatoes to the arugula, then divide the mixture between the four chicken breasts.

Tomato and avocado salad topping

—Combine the avocado, cherry tomatoes, spring onions and coriander in a bowl. Dress with the olive oil and lime juice. Divide the salad between the four chicken breasts, and serve with additional lime wedges.

From **My Father's Daughter**
By Gwyneth Paltrow
Grand Central Publishing, £16.99

—ROAST BEEF, ROAST POTATOES AND DANIELLE'S FAVOURITE, CREAMED LEEKS

from Danielle and Gary Lineker
Serves 6

—Ingredients

For the roast beef

—1.6kg of boneless rump roast (pick an end cut with a lot of fat marbling)
—olive oil
—8 slivers of garlic
—salt and pepper

For the potatoes

—6 large potatoes, peeled and quartered
—8 tbsp duck fat or other fat reserved for roasting
—pinch of salt

For the gravy

—red wine, water, and or beef stock
—corn starch

For the leeks

—knob of butter
—4 leeks
—4 tbsp double cream

—Method

—Start with the roast at room temperature (remove from refrigerator 1 hour before cooking – keep it wrapped). Preheat the oven to 190°C.

—With a sharp knife make eight small incisions around the roast. Place a sliver of garlic into each incision. Take a tbsp or so of olive oil and spread all around the roast. Sprinkle around the roast with salt and pepper. Place the roast directly on an oven rack, fatty side up, with a drip pan on a rack beneath the roasting rack. This arrangement creates convection in the oven so that you do not need to turn the roast. The roast is placed fat side up so that as the fat melts it will bathe the entire roast in its juices.

—Brown the roast at 190°C for half an hour. Lower the heat to 110°C. The roast should take somewhere from 2 to 3 hours additionally to cook. When the roast just starts to drip its juices and is brown on the outside, check the temperature with a meat thermometer. Pull the roast from the oven when the inside temperature of the roast is 57-60°C. Let the roast rest for at least 15 minutes, tented in aluminum foil to keep warm, before carving to serve.

To make the gravy

—Remove the dripping pan from the oven and place on the stove top at medium heat. Add some water, red wine or beef stock to the drippings to deglaze. Dissolve 1 tbsp of cornstarch in a little water and add to the drip pan. Stir quickly while the gravy thickens to avoid lumping. You can add a little butter if there is not a lot of fat in the drippings. Add salt and pepper to taste.

For the potatoes

—Place the potatoes in a large saucepan and just cover with cold water. Bring to the boil then boil, uncovered, for 7-8 minutes.

—Meanwhile, switch the oven to 220°C and place the oil or fat in a large roasting tin towards the top of the oven to heat thoroughly.

—Drain the potatoes thoroughly. Return them to the pan and shake vigorously.

—Take the tin from the oven and add the potatoes. Turn them quickly in the fat then cook at the top of the oven for 50-60 minutes, turning once halfway through cooking until crisp and golden on the outside and soft in the centre.

For the leeks

—Heat the butter in a pan, tip in the leeks and sweat until softened, but not coloured. Stir in the cream and cook for a further 2 minutes. Season to taste with salt and pepper.

—PASTA CARBONARA
by Kimberley Wyatt
Serves 2

—Ingredients
—250g spaghetti
—butter
—6 rashers streaky bacon, chopped
—6 brown cap mushrooms, sliced
—1 egg
—1 egg white
—25g parmesan, finely grated

—Method
—Boil the pasta. Crack the egg into a bowl, add the egg white, and beat. Season with salt and pepper. Add parmesan cheese.
—Meanwhile, fry the bacon and mushrooms. Use tongs to take the spaghetti out of the water and place in the bowl with the egg so that the egg cooks with the heat of the spaghetti.
—Add your bacon and mushrooms.

—SEARED BLACK BREAM WITH ROASTED AUBERGINE, TOMATO AND POTATO CRUSH AND KACHUMBER

from Vivek Singh, The Cinnamon Club

Serves 4

CINNAMON CLUB
VIVEK SINGH

—SEARED BLACK BREAM WITH ROASTED AUBERGINE, TOMATO AND POTATO CRUSH AND KACHUMBER

from Vivek Singh, The Cinnamon Club
Serves 4

"I love this dish for its simplicity. The aubergine crush and kachumber are probably two of the most familiar Indian accompaniments and might be considered mundane in some circumstances, but the combination with a simple fried fillet of bream is stunning. It's a great dish for entertaining, as much of it can be prepared in advance."

—Ingredients

—4 black bream fillets (or any white fish), pin-boned
—1 tablespoon vegetable or corn oil
—1 quantity of roasted aubergine, tomato and potato crush

For the kachumber

—¼ small cucumber, deseeded and cut into 3mm dice
—1 tomato, deseeded and cut into 3mm dice
—1 tsp salt
—1 tsp sugar
—juice of 1 lemon
—2 tbsp good olive oil
—1 tbsp finely chopped fresh coriander

For the marinade

—1 tsp salt
—½ tsp fennel seeds
—½ tsp black onion seeds
—½ tsp red chilli flakes

—Method

—First make the kachumber. Place the diced cucumber, carrot and tomato in a mixing bowl. Whisk together the salt, sugar, lemon juice, olive oil and coriander to make a dressing and mix it with the diced vegetables. Check the seasoning.
—Mix together all the ingredients for the marinade, rub them over the fish and set aside for 10 minutes.
—Heat the oil in a large, non-stick frying pan, add the black bream fillets, skin-side down, and sear for 3-4 minutes, until well coloured underneath. Turn and cook for another 2 minutes or until just cooked through.
—To serve, place the roasted aubergine, tomato and potato crush in the centre of each plate and put the fish on top, then drizzle the kachumber around the plate.

—CHESTNUT AND VEGETABLE BURGERS

from Carol Vorderman
Serves 8

—Ingredients

—125g couscous
—150ml hot vegetable stock
—1 tbsp extra virgin olive oil
—1 onion, finely chopped
—2 carrots, grated
—1 courgette, finely diced
—200g dried chestnut pieces
—1 egg, beaten
—3 tbsp chopped chives
—a little low-sodium salt and freshly ground black pepper
—extra olive oil for brushing

—Method

—Place the couscous in a bowl. Pour over the hot stock and leave to stand for 15 minutes until the stock has been absorbed.
—Meanwhile, heat the oil in a frying pan and cook the onion over a moderate heat for 5 minutes. Add the carrot and courgette and continue cooking for 5 minutes. Remove from the heat.
—Add the chestnuts, couscous, egg, chives and seasoning.
—Mix well.
—Divide the mixture into eight and firmly press into burger shapes. Chill until ready to serve.
—Heat the grill. Place the burgers on a grill tray, brush with a little olive oil then cook for about 15 minutes, turning carefully halfway through the cooking time.

Health statistics

—Chestnuts are low in fat and provide potassium, B-vitamins and vitamin E. Couscous supplies complex carbohydrates and the carrots are super-rich in betacarotene, a powerful antioxidant that helps protect against cancer and heart disease.

"BEING INVOLVED HAS GIVEN ME FIRSTHAND EXPERIENCE OF THE WONDERFUL WORK THE CHARITY DOES EVERY DAY."

orraine Pascale

—THE SKINNY TART

from Lorraine Pascale
Makes 8 tarts

"So there's a smidgeon of butter on, and in, the pastry, but otherwise these fruity little minxes are a rare guilt-free treat and if you get a wriggle on they can be made in under an hour. Impeccable."

—Ingredients

—80g butter, melted and cooled, plus extra for greasing
—270g shop-bought filo pastry
—4 tbsp apricot jam
—500g low or no fat Greek yoghurt
—2 tbsp honey
—seeds of 1 vanilla pod or 2 drops of vanilla extract
—1 small bunch black seedless grapes, halved
—1 bunch redcurrants
—1 dragon fruit, peeled and cubed
—2 large figs, quartered

The equipment

—12-hole muffin tin or cupcake tin

From **Baking Made Easy**
By Lorraine Pascale
HarperCollins, £18.99

—Method

—Preheat the oven to 180°C with the middle shelf ready. Grease the muffin or cupcake tin well.
—Cut the filo pastry into squares that are big enough to fit into the muffin holes and hang over the sides a little. Brush each piece of filo with lots of melted butter to stop them from burning in the oven, then push a filo square into a hole and add another filo square, you will need to layer up 3 or 4 pieces. Repeat until you have eight holes filled.
—Place the filo cases into the oven for 5 minutes or so, giving them time to crisp up. Once they look golden brown and crispy remove them from the oven and leave to cool for 10 minutes or so. Remove them from the muffin tray and place them on serving dishes. I always tend to break at least one when I take them out!
—Put the jam in a small pan and heat gently until warm.
—Mix the Greek yoghurt, honey and vanilla together in a bowl then place a good dollop into each pastry case. Now divide the fruit among the tartlets, piling it up high. Brush with the warm apricot jam to make a shiny glaze and serve. You can make all the component parts ahead of time and assemble the tarts at the last minute.
—You can also decorate with a sprig of fresh mint, or get creative with some raspberry jam thinned and well mixed with some water and drizzled on the plate for a touch of old-school food glamour.

—APPLE AND CINNAMON MUFFINS

from James Martin
Makes 6

—Ingredients

—1 egg, beaten
—40g caster sugar
—120ml milk
—50g butter, melted
—150g plain flour
—1½ tsp baking powder
—¼ tsp salt
—½ tsp ground cinnamon
—2 eating apples, peeled, cored and finely chopped

Topping

—12 brown sugar cubes, roughly chopped
—1 tsp ground cinnamon

—Method

—Pre-heat the oven to 200°C. Line a mini muffin tin with paper cases. Mix the egg sugar, milk and melted butter in a large bowl. Sift in the flour, baking powder, sal and cinnamon. Add the chopped apple and mix roughly.

—Spoon the mixture into the pre-preparec muffin cases. Make the topping by mixing the crushed sugar cubes with the cinnamon. Sprinkle over the uncooked muffins. Bake for 30-35 minutes until well risen and golden. Cool on a wire rack.

—JOLLOF RICE WITH CHICKEN

from Melvin Odoom
Serves 4

—Ingredients

—8 skinless, boneless chicken thighs, cut into large pieces
—3 tbsp vegetable or sunflower oil
—1 large onion, halved and sliced
—3 tbsp tomato purée
—1 chicken stock cube
—400g basmati rice
—1 red pepper, deseeded and thickly sliced
—1 yellow pepper, deseeded and thickly sliced
—100g okra, halved
—bunch of coriander, roughly chopped

For the ginger and chilli base

—2 garlic cloves
—2 x 400g cans plum tomatoes
—thumb-size piece fresh root ginger
—1 scotch bonnet chilli, deseeded

—Method

—Season the chicken with salt and pepper. Heat 2 tbsp of the oil in a large, deep frying pan over a high heat then add the meat and fry for about 5 minutes until golden all over. Lift out of the pan and onto a plate.

—Add the rest of the oil to the pan and fry the onions until soft but not golden, about 5 minutes. While the onions cook, make the ginger and chilli base. Put the garlic, tomatoes, ginger and chilli into a food processor or blender and whizz until smooth.

—Add the tomato purée to the onions, fry for another 2 minutes, then add the ginger and chilli mix. Crumble in the stock cube, stir, then pour in 600ml boiling water. Add the chicken, bring to the boil then simmer for 15 minutes.

—Put the rice into a large bowl, cover with cold water and use your hands to wash the grains. Tip the water out then repeat twice until the water runs clear. Add the rice to the pan, turn the heat down to a simmer then cover with foil and a lid (so no steam can escape) and cook for 20 minutes.

—Take the lid off (the rice won't be cooked yet) then scatter the peppers and okra over the rice. Re-cover and cook for 10 minutes until the vegetables are softened and the rice tender. Just before serving, mix the vegetables through and scatter with coriander.

—BAKED EGG CUSTARD TART

from Marcus Wareing
Makes 8 tarts

—Ingredients

For the pastry

—225g flour, plus extra for dusting
—1 pinch salt
—1 lemon, zest only
—150g butter
—75g caster sugar
—1 free range egg yolk
—1 free range egg

For the custard filling

—9 free range egg yolks
—75g caster sugar
—500ml whipping cream
—2 nutmegs

—Method

—Preheat the oven to 170°C.

—For the pastry, rub together the flour, salt, lemon zest and butter until the mixture resembles breadcrumbs. Add the sugar, then beat together the egg yolk and whole egg and slowly add these, mixing until the pastry forms a ball. Wrap tightly in cling film and refrigerate for 2 hours.

—Roll out the pastry on a lightly floured surface to 2mm thickness. Use to line an 18cm flan ring placed on a baking sheet. Line with greaseproof paper and fill with baking beans, then bake blind for about 10 minutes or until the pastry is starting to turn golden brown. Remove the paper and beans, and allow to cool.

—Turn the oven down to 130°C.

—For the filling, bring the cream to the boil. Whisk the yolks and sugar together then add the cream and mix well. Pass the mixture through a fine sieve into a jug.

—Place the pastry case in the oven then pour the custard mix right to the brim. Grate the nutmeg liberally over the top then bake for 30-40 minutes or until the custard appears set but not too firm. Remove from the oven and allow to cool to room temperature before serving.

—RASPBERRY & LEMON TORTA

from Tana Ramsay
Serves 8

"This is at its delicious best when served slightly warm. It does sink a little in the middle but this recipe is all about taste, not looks. It will last a couple of days, which is always handy. And I do just love raspberries!"

—**RASPBERRY & LEMON TORTA**
from Tana Ramsay
Serves 8

—**Ingredients**

—115g unsalted butter, gently melted and cooled, plus more for the tin
—450g raspberries
—juice of ½ lemon
—225g golden caster sugar, plus more for the top
—3 free range eggs
—250g plain flour, sifted
—2 rounded tsp baking powder
—finely grated zest of 1 unwaxed lemon

—Preheat the oven to 160°C. Butter a 20cm round cake tin and line the base with baking parchment.
—Place the raspberries and lemon juice into a mixing bowl. In another large bowl, whisk together the sugar and eggs until pale and thick, then carefully fold in the flour, baking powder and lemon zest. Gently stir in the butter.
—Tip the batter into the tin then scatter in the raspberries and their juices. Sprinkle a little sugar over the top.
—Bake for 1 hour, or until it springs back to the touch (see Tana's Kitchen Secret, below). Check halfway through the cooking time – you may find you need to cover the torta with foil to prevent the top from scorching. Allow to cool in the tin, then turn out.

How to know when a cake is cooked

—The cake will have an even colour, be firm yet springy to the touch and should be slightly shrinking away from the edges of the tin. Insert a clean skewer right down into the centre. If it comes out clean, the cake is cooked. After removing from the oven, give it a few minutes to rest in its tin before turning out on a cooling rack.

From **Tana's Kitchen Secrets**
By Tana Ramsay
Mitchell Beazley, £19.99

—SAFFRON POACHED PEARS WITH CHOCOLATE MOUSSE

from Jun Tanaka, Pearl
Serves 4

—SAFFRON POACHED PEARS WITH CHOCOLATE MOUSSE

from Jun Tanaka, Pearl
Serves 4

—Ingredients

The pears

—4 ripe pears, peeled and seeds taken out with a parisien
—750ml white wine
—200g caster sugar
—½ lemon
—1 pinch saffron
—1 vanilla pod
—1 sprig mint

The chocolate mousse

—200g dark chocolate
—80ml milk
—1 yolk
—4 egg whites
—20g caster sugar

—Method

—Add all the ingredients for the pears into a pan, bring to the boil, add the pears and take off the heat. Leave to cool down. This is best done a few hours in advance.
—Place the chocolate in a metal bowl and place on a pan of simmering water until melted.
—Boil the milk and add to the chocolate. Whisk in the egg yolk.
—Whisk the egg white and sugar until soft peaks. Add a third of the whites to the chocolate and whisk in. Fold in the rest. Pour into a container and set in the fridge for 20 minutes.
—To serve, dip a spoon into melted chocolate and flick onto a plate to obtain a streak. Place a pear in the centre and spoon on the chocolate mousse.
—Finish with a sprig of mint.

—BREAD AND BUTTER PUDDING

from Gary Rhodes

Serves 6-8

—BREAD AND BUTTER PUDDING

from Gary Rhodes
Serves 6-8

—Ingredients

—1 x 1.5-1.8 litre pudding basin, buttered
—12 medium slices white bread, crusts cut off
—50g unsalted butter, softened
—1 vanilla pod or few drops of vanilla essence
—400ml double cream
—400ml milk
—8 egg yolks
—175g caster sugar, plus extra for the caramelised topping
—25g sultanas
—25g raisins

—Method

—Pre-heat the oven to 180°C.
—Butter the bread. Split the vanilla pod and place in a saucepan with the cream and milk and bring to the boil. While it is heating, whisk together the egg yolks and caster sugar in a bowl. Allow the cream mix to cool a little, then strain it onto the egg yolks, stirring all the time. You now have the custard.
—Cut the bread into triangular quarters or halves, and arrange in the dish in three layers, sprinkling the fruit between two layers and leaving the top clear. Now pour over the warm custard, lightly pressing the bread to help it soak in, and leave it to stand for at least 20-30 minutes before cooking to ensure that the bread absorbs all the custard.
—The pudding can be prepared to this stage several hours in advance and cooked when needed. Place the dish in a roasting tray three-quarters filled with warm water and bake for 20-30 minutes until the pudding begins to set. Don't overcook it or the custard will scramble. Remove the pudding from the water bath, sprinkle it liberally with caster sugar and glaze under the grill on a medium heat or with a gas gun to a crunchy golden finish.
—When glazing, the sugar dissolves and caramelises, and you may find that the corners of the bread begin to burn. This helps the flavour, giving a bittersweet taste that mellows when it is eaten with the rich custard, which seeps out of the wonderful bread sponge when you cut into it.

—MIXED FRUIT PAVLOVA

from Emma Bunton
Serves 6

—Ingredients

For the pavlova base

—2 tsp cornflour
—2 tsp white wine vinegar
—1 tsp vanilla extract
—4 medium free range eggs, at room temperature
—200g caster sugar

For the topping

—450g fresh strawberries, washed and hulled
—250g fresh raspberries, washed
—1 tbsp icing sugar
—284ml carton double cream

—Method

—Preheat the oven to 140°C. Line a baking sheet with non-stick baking parchment, cutting it to fit. Using a cake tin or plate as a template, draw a 23cm diameter circle on the parchment with a pencil.

—Place the cornflour, vinegar and vanilla extract in a small bowl and blend with a teaspoon until smooth. Separate the eggs one at a time, taking care not to include any yolks with the whites. As each egg is separated, tip the white into the large mixing bowl.

—Whisk the egg whites until they are stiff enough to hold their shape. Whisk in the sugar a tablespoon at a time, adding a little of the cornflour mixture each time. When all the sugar and cornflour has been added, the consistency of the mixture will be thick and marshmallowy.

—Using the spatula, turn the meringue mixture onto the baking sheet. Spread it to the marked line, then swirl with the spatula, making a slight indentation in the centre for the filling. Bake for 1 hour, then turn the oven off and leave the pavlova base to cool completely in the oven.

—Place 100g each of the strawberries and raspberries in a liquidiser or food processor and blend until fairly smooth. Press through a sieve into a bowl to remove the seeds. Stir in the icing sugar. Slice or halve the remaining strawberries, depending on their size.

—Pour the cream into a large bowl and whip with a whisk until it just holds its shape. Take care not to overwhip the cream or it will become dull and grainy. Using a fish slice or wide spatula, carefully remove the pavlova from the paper and transfer to a flat serving plate. Spoon the cream into the centre, spreading it out a little. Pile the remaining fruit on top and drizzle with a little of the fruit sauce. The remaining sauce can be served in a jug.

—DELIA'S BANANA AND WALNUT LOAF

from Delia Smith
Serves 8

"This is a lovely, moist cake that keeps well and is perfect for picnics or packed lunches. In the summer it's brilliant served cut in thick slices and spread with clotted cream."

—Ingredients

—4 medium bananas (approximately 350g)
—170g walnut pieces
—1 pinch of salt
—1 rounded tsp baking powder
—1 level tsp ground cinnamon
—110g plain flour
—110g wholewheat flour
—grated zest 1 orange
—grated zest 1 lemon
—110g butter at room temperature
—175g soft dark brown sugar
—2 large eggs at room temperature

For the topping
—1 level tbsp demerara sugar

rom **How to Cook Book One**
y Delia Smith
BC Books, £20

rom **Delia's Vegetarian Collection**
y Delia Smith
BC Books, £25

—Method

—Pre-heat the oven to 180°C.
—Begin, as soon as the oven has pre-heated, by spreading the nuts out on a baking sheet and toasting them lightly in the oven for 7-8 minutes – use a timer so that you don't forget them. After that, remove them from the oven to a chopping board, let them cool briefly, then chop them fairly roughly. Now, in a bowl, peel and mash three of the bananas to a purée with a fork, and peel and chop the other one into 1 cm chunks.
—Next you need to take a large mixing bowl and sift the salt, baking powder, cinnamon and both the flours into it, holding the sieve up high to give it a good airing, then adding the bran that's left in the sieve. Now simply add all the remaining ingredients (except the chopped banana and nuts) and, using an electric hand whisk, begin to beat the mixture, first on a slow speed for about half a minute, then increasing the speed to mix everything thoroughly and smoothly. Then lightly fold in the chopped banana and walnuts. You may need to add a drop of milk to give a mixture that drops easily off a spoon when you give it a sharp tap on the side of the bowl.
—Next pile the mixture into the tin, level the top with the back of a spoon and sprinkle on the demerara sugar. Bake in the centre of the oven for 1¼-1½ hours, until the cake feels springy in the centre.
—After that, remove it from the oven and let it cool for about 5 minutes before turning it out on to a wire tray. Then let it get completely cold before serving or transferring it to a cake tin.

—CHOCOLATE MILK CUPCAKES

by Fearne Cotton
Makes 16

—CHOCOLATE MILK CUPCAKES

by Fearne Cotton
Makes 16

—Ingredients

For the cake

- —100g dark/bitter sweet chocolate
- —175g unsalted butter, cubed
- —225g caster sugar
- —4 eggs
- —100g self raising flour
- —2½ tbsp cocoa powder
- —1 pinch salt
- —chocolate sprinkles to top
- —edible glitter to dust (optional)

For vanilla butter cream

- —120g butter, cubed
- —500g icing sugar
- —1 tsp vanilla extract
- —1 tbsp milk

Recipe and image kindly donated by **Lola's Kitchen**
lolas-kitchen.co.uk

—Method

- —Muffin pan lined with 12 muffin cases.
- —Preheat the oven to 180°C.
- —Put the chocolate and butter in a heatproof bowl over a pan of simmering water. Do not let the base of the bowl touch the water! Heat, stirring until the chocolate melts and you have a smooth glossy mixture. Remove from the heat and stir in the sugar. Leave to cool for 10 minutes.
- —Now beat with an electric hand mixer for 3 minutes. Add the eggs, one at a time, beating for 10 seconds between each addition. Sift the flour, cocoa and salt into the bowl and beat until blended.
- —Divide the mixture between muffin cases. Bake in the preheated oven for 20-25 minutes or until well risen and a skewer inserted comes out clean. Remove from the oven and leave to cool completely on a wire rack before decorating.

Vanilla butter cream

- —While the cupcakes are cooling down make the vanilla buttercream.
- —Put the butter in a bowl and beat with an electric hand mixer until very soft and smooth. Sift half the sugar into the bowl, beating until incorporated. Add the second half of the sugar and beat on a low speed. Add the vanilla.
- —Slowly pour in the milk and when it is mixed in, beat for 3-5 minutes on a higher speed.
- —Spread the frosting over the cold cupcakes using a spatula, or spoon the frosting into a piping bag fitted with a start nozzle/tip and pipe it on top of the cupcakes. Decorate with chocolate sprinkles and dust with edible glitter.

—SMARTIE COOKIES (BECAUSE SMARTIES MAKE YOU SMART!)

from Helena Bonham Carter
Serves 8

—Ingredients

—350g flour
—1 tsp bicarbonate of soda
—1 tsp salt
—225g butter or margerine
—175g caster sugar
—175g soft brown sugar
—1 tsp vanilla extract
—2 eggs
—350g milk chocolate chips
—1 tube of Smarties (or more!)

—Method

—Preheat the oven to 190°C.
—In a bowl, mix the flour, baking soda and salt.
—In another bowl, beat the butter, caster sugar, brown sugar and vanilla extract until creamy. Beat in the eggs. Gently stir in the flour mixture. Stir in the chocolate chips.
—Split the dough into two halves, rolling each out into sausage shapes, approximately 5cm in diameter. Wrap them in cling film and transfer to the fridge until ready to use.
—When you are ready to bake the cookies, simply cut the log into slices 2cm thick and lay on a baking tray, widely spaced apart and decorate with the Smarties. Bake for 9-11 minutes.
—Serve.

—ICED RED BERRY SOUFFLÉ

by Michel Roux Jr
Serves 10

—ICED RED BERRY SOUFFLÉ
from Michel Roux Jr
Serves 10

—Ingredients
—1kg mixed berries (e.g. strawberries, raspberries, blueberries, blackcurrants), and extra to decorate
—400g egg whites
—500ml water
—80ml whipping cream

—Method
—Hull and, if necessary, wash the fruit. Blend with 150g of the sugar, then pass through a fine sieve and add lemon juice to heighten the taste if required. Prepare 10 individual soufflé dishes (9cm diameter x 6cm deep) by tying a piece of greaseproof paper around the edge to form a collar that stands 5cm above the rim.
—Put the egg whites into the bowl of an electric mixer. In a perfectly clean saucepan, dissolve the remaining 250g of sugar in the water over low heat. When the sugar is completely dissolved, bring to the boil, skim off the foam and cook to 120°C on a sugar thermometer. Beat the egg whites until foamy, then, with the whisk still running, pour the hot sugar directly on the egg whites, avoiding the beaters. Continue beating until the meringue is cool.
—Whip the cream until soft peaks form and fold into the fruit pulp. Delicately fold in the meringue, then spoon into the prepared soufflé dishes. Freeze for 12 hours.
—Decorate with fresh berries and, if you like, serve with a sauce made by pureeing 500g berries with 100g caster sugar, sharpening the taste with a little lemon juice.

rom **Le Gavroche Cookbook**
y Michel Roux Jr
V&N, £25

—APPLE CRUMBLE

from Myleene Klass
Serves 6

"My favourite dessert is apple crumble. It must be served with custard!"

—Ingredients

Best ever crumble topping

- —170g flour
- —60g porridge oats
- —225g demerara sugar
- —170g unsalted butter, chilled and cubed

Filling

- —400g cooking apples, peeled, cored and quartered
- —50g sugar, to sweeten
- —1 tbsp water

—Method

- —Mix together the flour, oats and sugar and rub in butter or blitz all the ingredients in a food processor for a few seconds.

Filling

- —Cook the apples for approximately 5 minutes.
- —Put the cooked apples in an oven proof dish allow the mixture to cool then spread the topping on top.
- —Cook at 175°C for around 35 minutes until the topping is golden and crisp.

—LEMON POSSET

from Phil Vickery
Serves 4-6

—Ingredients

—397g can condensed milk
—150ml double cream
—finely grated zest and juice of 4 large lemons (about 150ml)
—1 tbsp chopped mint leaves
—1 tsp granulated sugar
—squeeze of lemon juice

—Method

—Whisk the condensed milk and cream together until thick and very light; 4 or 5 minutes.
—Add the lemon juice and zest and whip for a few seconds only, as the mixture will thicken very quickly.
—Spoon the lemon cream into ramekins, or a large trifle bowl and then chill for at least an hour, or overnight.
—To serve, muddle the mint leaves with the sugar and lemon juice and sprinkle a little onto the lemon cream.

“WE’VE MET SOME AMAZING CHILDREN THROUGH WORKING WITH RAYS OF SUNSHINE, AND FEEL HONOURED TO BE IN A POSITION TO HELP. THE CHARITY GIVES THOUSANDS OF SERIOUSLY ILL KIDS THE CHANCE TO TAKE TIME OUT AND HAVE SOME FUN AND WE ARE DELIGHTED TO HELP WHEREVER WE CAN.”

One Direction